Consider the Snail

Peter Hansen

Consider the Snail

Consider the Snail
ISBN 978 1 76041 094 0
Copyright © text Peter Hansen 2016
Cover image © viperagp – Fotolia.com

First published 2016 by
GINNINDERRA PRESS
PO Box 3461 Port Adelaide 5015 Australia
www.ginninderrapress.com.au

Contents

Consider the snail	9
40 Degrees	11
The Heifer Calving	12
Day's End, After Crutching	13
Agistment Sheep, Autumn Quambone	14
An Offering	15
Early March	16
La Nina	17
Showering, the Shearers Huts, Thargonmindah	19
The Budgerigar in the Classroom	20
The Drought Breaks, July 2010	21
The Rabbit Shooter	22
The Rabbit Shooter Reprise	23
From Chute Number Three, the Death of the Bull	24
Broken	26
Dishonesty	27
A Distress	28
Zara Station	29
The Goat Yards, Arcadia, Wanaaring, Queensland	30
The Heron	31
At the Gate	32
In My Hearing	34
For the Shepherds to Come	36
The Narrows, East London	37
Wednesday Afternoon	38
First Winter's Night, London	40
Saturday Morning, Epsom	41
Easter Weekend	42
The James I Bible	43
In the High Street	44
Stamford Hill and Radio 4	45

Exmoor	46
Moray Firth, April	47
Iona	48
From the Lakes	49
A Visit to Cambridge	50
Monmouth	51
Above the gorse	52
The Dead Mole	53
Passing Traffic	54
Skoma Island	55
Passing the Baptist Chapel	56
The Maiden Ewe	57
Laugharne	58
Carmarthen to Llandeilo	59
Wool Pressing, Wales	60
Cymru Bull	61
Finding the Words	62
The Wombat Hole Reprise	65
Coming Home	67
Thunderstorms are	69
Today	71
The boy has his hair in a bun	72
Melbourne, The CBD	74
In September	77
Outside are odd things	78
Along the Yarra	80
Victoria Gardens, Abbotsford	81
The Yarra Bank	82
For my nephew	83
The Crossing	84
Studley Park Night-time	85
Horse Riding for the Disabled. Carpe Diem	86
First Placement in Aged Care	87

'Thou giv'st the ass his hide, the snail his shell'
                Robbie Burns, 'A Poem In Embryo'

Consider the snail

Consider the snail,
as if by chance the sun,
or by design
light, strikes
through leaves wrought, rung
boisterous
catches silver,
necklaced dots, a glance
of glistening,
a casual feint disdaining straight away
that border a path contrives,
with a shining, dreaming
sweep of a songline trace
of passing,
vanished, like Leichhardt.

Contemplate the spiderling
casting lace web
in shocking wind, anchored escape,
frantic dew jewelled,
flying decoration, abandoning hope,
reconciliation
now impossible,
for this is spring,
infanticide
rides on morning sun.

Making love
I wish the passing dragonfly good luck
knowing he has but hours to find a mate
and copulate,
to place his organ in her head,
fall in love with her mind,
or failing that, explode
in iridescent green and gold,
wonderfully unrequited
across my windscreen.

40 Degrees

You have no idea,
one day perhaps, not now.
Did you notice the ants,
in the heat, scurry, good word scurry,
scurry across the cement in the heat,
too hot on their black backs,
or too hot underfoot,
geddit, hot ants feet, ha, ha,
comically casting industry aside
in headlong pursuit of, well, industry?
You have no idea,
no one gets used to it, ever.
Not even ants.

The Heifer Calving

Birth fluid like honey
runs arms-length from the drowning,
contractions set hard
on seeking in the dark
with chains and hooks,
white cotton rope,
like setting a sail,
tongue-lolling head slippery and larded,
a cross-channel swimmer;
goggled with membrane
pinned by juvenile hips,
two forms untimely held
in urgency failing, like light
until from despair
the diver emerges,
splashes to earth,
breathless,
and in that moment
caught between birth and death,
heaven and hell
the heifer rents the sky
with a moan of pain or loss.

Day's End, After Crutching

What drunkenness is this that cannot sleep
or in its cups find peace or rest?
Carpal Tunnel, a deep, black uncertainty,
neither pain nor cramp,
disrupts sleep on the shearer's cot
shared with mice and swallow nest.
What intoxication is carried by dreams of grape
that in the gaze of summer yearns to fill
but in failed fruitfulness dies a shrunken purple?
It is a nervous dance along the arm,
insistent spasm in the palm
like a half-recalled affair, passing and hurtful.
What desire is this that falls and lies wasted
at the root of the vine,
conjured by the constant pull and drive of handpiece,
fist driving into flank,
courting all that pass with the heady smell
of season's rotting?
What questions are these, that in their wakefulness
rouse and trouble?
So the toes point like a ballerina's
and the leg is undressed from woollen hosiery
in a falling shower of white locks.

Agistment Sheep, Autumn Quambone

In earaching stillness
daybreak
clatters shrikes, magpie warbles
dance the flat box creeks,
dying frost falls, drops Mitchell grass,
drips gate hinges
snatch an intake of breath
when full moon, idle overnight,
fills dawn with marriage to a sun
recently lost,
caught somewhere between summer and winter,
where hoggets march rank
and file pad to water,
steam rising from shanks,
pin-rush bore-drain edges
patrolled by draft of ibis
and always, always a solitary crane.

An Offering

Brindle goat,
of late my words carry little colour,
so, as I slit your neck
can I find in sacrifice,
rose blood, pink-blush throat
hues of evisceration,
once brilliant in the pulse of heartbeat?
Or blue jeans stained, purple,
regally stuck with golden fat,
brown-white kemp,
shed in easy rain from your hide,
a conflagration of green flies, black ants,
a rainbow of your humours
on the whet of my knife?

Early March

Sweet and gentle breeze
I am not beguiled by your touch,
of soft and dappled sun,
do not seduce me with your smile,
song-filled, swaying days,
do not to court me with your dance
because we have met before
and I have felt your bitter grasp
of winter winds, dried and died
under the summer of a yellow stare,
and been too easily dismissed
by your full card of partners.

La Nina

rises unexpectedly
in passion of thunderheads,
murmurings that in their intensity
draw tears from wounds and memories,
aches plumbed from wells of desire
run rivers of sweat in thickening,
sky-wasted lace of light.
The lizard knows neither the time
nor the place of the coming,
he notes the heat, perhaps the wind
but cannot feel the pressure drop
in the scaly holes behind his head,
to be caught in such violence
that death becomes him mid-stride,
frozen in form to startle my passing.

At smoko she joked, You may see me shear,
but you'll never see me crutch.

the pretty,
the blonde on three,
the Kiwi Pakeha
décolleté,
with decorated cleavage,
butterflies, always butterflies,
hair in neat halo
smiles
in manner so disarming
that the lousy ewe
kicking the Christ out of her Adam's rib
will,
eventually,
know
it has met its match.

Showering, the Shearers Huts, Thargomindah

Green frogs sit, and blink,
blink and sit,
dozens, extras
in a B-grade horror film.
The shower rose spits, starts,
spits and runs
hot and cold
needles make me dance
in sulphur's stench,
bore water,
soap and scoured lanoline
runs my legs in blackened tracks
past weeping scars
of mulga stakes
and greasy scum,
around my feet,
gets deeper, and croaks.

The Budgerigar in the Classroom

A bird in close intensity with its reflection,
a green study of solemnity and introspection
tilts its head slyly at the spinning, silver shining
mirror and nods wryly, or is that simply mining

the image far too much, for it is only
a bird in a cage and as such to describe *lonely*
is a construct made from, was it years of observation,
when flocks tore through the scrub in regular conflation,

teeming with each other in full and raucous song,
but I would rather, this creature, held too long
could take to the air and the desert would ring
without classroom chatter, and the thing
which had made it whole would fly again.

The Drought Breaks, July 2010

Again clouds balloon the sky
Restoration ladies lifting swelled skirts
to piss in casual passing
on the mud-running gutter of creeks.
Daisies dash the plain
and dribble the fence songlines
from paddock to paddock,
white-capped and yellow-eyed
they dance through saltbush
fecund with the smile of spring.
A growth of moss has purpled over claypans,
flanked by ranks
silver-breasted rye and careless copper-burr,
where in depression a black thistle feeds,
the felted yellow bones of a ewe and lamb.

The Rabbit Shooter

For forty years,
a working life,
this beam swings
back
and
forth,
making light in the black
of love and lack,
and shadows, fear and longing
casually exposed
by the arc
a spot
in
gentle
pendulum
restless for it falls,
in fierce and blinding,
on the trapped, unblinking
frozen, immobile,
that, in spite of a racing heart and frantic mind,
welcomes the whisper shot of mortality.

The Rabbit Shooter Reprise

Still,
stock still.
Lock stock and barrel still.
Wide-eyed still,
heart fast beating races still,
flight fight fear and fucking still,
still and waiting,
forever waiting,
this catalogue, a life of waiting still
and struggling,
struggling with
heart fast beating races still,
flight fight fear and fucking still,
lock stock and barrel.

From Chute Number Three, the Death of the Bull

The bull is between my thighs,
he strains and shudders,
exhaling with a deepness
that crushes my legs
and on the counter breath
thick plaited rope
is snatched tighter
making us one.
Spur steel slides down
behind the Minotaur head
striking a single note
from the bell below his belly;
I hear the breathing of ants
track across the gate
as it opens into a chasm,
and we are as one.

Scrotum shrivelled
I am pithed, cast and rotting
windfall, discontent
of flies cloud my eyes,
crows in curious sentiment
shrouded black and cawling,
toll in mournful bell
I swell, I swell,
let slow bubbles of breathing
break from nostril,
run down a tongue,
long, fat, idiot drooling
with pain filling
every shudder breaking
spastic thrashing
stills, in heartbeat quick
rifle cocking,
failing in this red veil
to summon a bellowing
which once so defined me.

Broken

my nails are broken,
not all of them,
not on a cross
nor misshapen by a hammer,
just the toes,
hard, as if cast in a furnace,
splintered, as if cooled too soon,
uncommon thick, fashioned by a novice,
bent grotesque
as archeological detritus,
are my outrage, my spoliation,
wounds gathered
in constant cloven-hoofed passing
that in carelessness, or spite,
stood and twisted their heavy
or countless small and vicious feet
across my boots, insufficient
to provide respite for forty years,
days, nights in wilderness.

Dishonesty

To lie and lie is the habit
of lurchers and cattle dogs
spent from their copulation and industry,
chained to faint shade
in the common practice of their owners,
in the abandoned dust of horizon
out of reach of humanity,
and the deceit of a hock snap,
and the bite that greets, unheralded,
leaves the shadow of a smile on a muzzle
catching the scent, another bitch in heat.

In yard dogs.
the essence of the wolf
is barely hidden an animal
which herds and hunts the sheep in packs.
The muzzle is an artifice,
Venetian mask, which holds,
but does not hide desire, intent
when pressed deep in udders, flanks,
sometimes the throat and ears.
It is no love kiss
but a passion out of control.

A Distress

of kites
floats
cinder black
from
furnace
baked
red
clay,
whistle
death's song

in conclusion
in dismay

of locusts
ripe
for
the
taking
We
are the Revelation.

Zara Station

A clutch of guineafowl
perambulates, without economy,
in an earnestness of mathematic fellows,
heads up, heads down,
mindless of the lawn,
Please Keep Off Unless et cetera,
a gathering grey and black plumage of gowns
and frantic discourse,
ignorant of the watchful hush of kites
foaming above.

The Goat Yards, Arcadia, Wanaaring, Queensland

I am Pan,
I am orange-eyed and black-bearded
in weak, white, daybreak light.
I am heavy-horned and rampant,
in red-dust's halo
my musk has filled the air
and I piss and corrupt like Socrates.
I am Pan
in sinister raiment and wild desire,
I deprave the shepherds
and rattle gates of nymph and fawn,
make echoes that drive them to flight,
for I am Pan,
defiler of worlds,
victor at Olympus and Marathon,
Hear my cry.

The Heron

The heron thinks.
He is solitary.
I am solitary, he thinks,
up to his curiously formed ankle
in the frog thick damask rich
fetid reed-bed sludge,
I am alone
but for mating,
or a brief, curious stroll
with passing ibis.
Yet, he thinks,
taking to the air somnolent,
slowly
defying gravity,
I am never lonely.

At the Gate

The goanna prehistoric
eye blinks, not surprised,
disinterested, perhaps,
probably.
The goanna leans, very still,
front leg loosely cast
across the bottom rung
of a gate
like a man at a bar,
insouciant, casual,
looking somewhere
far away,
a middle distance
favoured by the drunk,
as a tongue tests
the air.
The goanna blinks, again,
with one, two eyelids,
sees the world differently,
perhaps,
probably.
I open the gate slowly
talking, can he hear,
who knows, snakes
can't,
see how sharp his talons
how dense his hide
how I have become
circumspect.

I drive the ute through the gate,
swing it back into place
and the goanna doesn't move,
at all,
stares at me unmoving,
a reptilian lollipop man
waiting for eternity.
I thank him.

In My Hearing

Disconnected, the windmill,
fills a midnight breeze,
calling in companion cry
steel on steel,
coal-black, desultory weeping
of rusted and pitted pipes
that in concordance
describe the sound
of a soul in disarray,
dashing dark into pieces
so uncomposed
wings of evening
are forced to fall, white-breasted,
grasping to a fence,
heaving, open-mouthed for air
which, in the heat of this moon,
comes uneasily.

So this is the proverb.
The owl cometh in silence
to menace in shape
beyond firelight
that in night
joins the jackal black
and is Jacob's curse, or worse
the wing'd whisperer
marks its place, calls despair,
betrays its race
in these deserts unseen
like gods between
sunrise and sunset
hovers, a nocturnal lover, harbinger of death,
perhaps too harsh an epithet
for one that cries,
Athena, I am here.

For the Shepherds to Come

'Et in Arcadia ego'
but it comes to this, death, a headstone,
even alone a point of repose
of greater comfort than those
it has been my custom to inhabit,
but do not believe in a place
without sorrow, sin,
or destruction
for there will be tears,
transgressions,
a host of fears without trace of tenderness,
so that which you care for will die,
bloat, wither, lie about fields
of sunny indifference,
dreams and ravens will fly
and the banality of this constant pasture
will not provide, nor will you find
what you are after.

The Narrows, East London

Into evening's death
of Whistler crane and towpath
this canal lies idle
but for heartbeat slow
rise and fall
of rubbish against the lock,
of gulls against the wave
a hollow wind made
light across the water empty as night,
bleak as love lost or denied,
cold as the graves in St Stephen's
that will have, hold, need,
this part of me,
washed in grey reflection
and dull disposition
along a river
to weep dreams
swept away by rushing
white-capped tide,
mocking idiocy and vanity
with purple raven call
cried on a blast
wrongly cold from the north,
the fading sun at odds
with my usual orientation
such as it was, once,
setting tears fast on my face
tight as hemp knots on bollards,
black as pitch hulls,
darker than sudden failing day.

Wednesday Afternoon

In Stoke Newington High Street
Lubavitch stride, earnest
as a rabbit might, Alice,
with clock, apron, scarf
as if the shops may close Sunday, forever, soon,
hats covered against rain by bespoke plastic
fastened with elastic, mindless of the falling hail,
just another test visited by Yahweh,
their wives, young, stout, fecund,
flat-heeled in flocks of black, perambulate,
serious as crows seldom seen
past the Common, silver
in rye-grass, yellow dandelions, daisies,
weeds that stain the meat, the milk
or would, if stock still grazed,
clover insufficient, small leafed,
small as tinned peas, small as cans of tonic,
packets of rice, packets of ten cigarettes
from the off licence, on the corner
rattling with unexpected exchange,
language too dense to countenance, to engage.

In Abney Cemetery and ruined church, 1868,
the final resting of Walter Thomas,
and belov'd wife,
surely it has not been two weeks,
the measure 'tween the headstones, caught
by the faintest whisper, spring
has burst the trees,
erupted plants without a name,
commonplace as herbage,
a derogatory
that suited country after drought so well,
with the first heat of summer,
young men, windows down music up
pass the crossing, hair too short for product,
seriously,
text me, text me,
buses, double-decked, swaying;
incongruent as pachyderms
are patient, wait
in rows to stop, move on, stop, move on
winding wren steepled lanes
to the bell of assembled mahouts.

First Winter's Night, London

At last the bells grip and toll,
fade and swell in winter wind,
ring Oranges and Lemons
in practised short order from St Anne's,
from Steniz Café Breakfast-Lunch-Dinner
and, finally, late afternoon, these streets
have become Conan Doyle sleets of darkness
beating from the east,
or, will I ever get my bearings right,
beating from the shuffling lights
of number 15 Bus, Canary Wharf or Hansom Cab,
Minicab, Drivers Wanted, Enquire Within,
I cross the traffic and reach for you.

Saturday Morning, Epsom

I have, at last, met the English crow,
which in manner, character, discourse
is so unlike my familiar of the western plains
and it struts and frets
in the habit of a puppet,
cast in Greenwich Dance Theatre
just last week,
a solitary form which, in its confidence,
parades the Stamford Green Park & Pond,
beak-look sharp in its understanding,
and so diffident, so confident, so approximating
in its shape the evil an antipodean cousin,
replete with tissue of eyes and string of kidneys
fails to fashion.

Easter Weekend

South Molton church Saturday morning
was empty
but for some brightly painted saints in the windows,
a gasping east wind,
and God,
in silence so complete
I was exposed,
and the sound of weeping hymns recalled
was no consolation,
having forsaken Friday,
being crucified elsewhere,
lost on Sunday seeking resurrection
or a bus to Exeter,
in cold so unforgiving
my soul begged release
which has yet to been found.

The James I Bible

Tickets by Invitation Only

I met Melvyn Bragg
in Henry's kitchen, Hampton Court.
I met Melvyn Bragge,
hors d 'oeuvres, a fire, white wine
in slight glasses,
in Henry's kitchen,
smaller than I remembered,
not Henry, nor the Court,
when he, not Henry,
and his hair, nodded, in passing,
mano-a-mano,
as courtiers might, would, should
so that later, in the Great Hall,
when the man of my imagination
was so casual and disinterested
I could have easily reached for my steel,
and we both would have been lost.

In the High Street

High crown hats worn
and sometimes cheap
chimney tops
fill and define
horizons
shoulder to shoulder
coal black
overwhelming,
strangely formed
hair strung
curiously curled
under balding pates
white shirts,
white socks,
prayer shawls
casually spread
across belly and ribs,
lamb not pork,
skullcaps, felt dark,
without elan
desperately the same
as bollards
by contrivance
or by accident
but charcoaled
like Ruben's sketches,
obscure as Rembrant figures,
all art is drawing
all religion is
religion.

Stamford Hill and Radio 4

Beyond the window,
across the rooftops welcomely hilled,
a tower erupts, a mosque,
apartments, a Victorian folly,
shining above congregations of ash and oak
fecund in spring sun, soporifically green and indolent
until caught by a passing breeze, northerly, southerly,
I can never determine the strange patterns of this country,
light, dark, skies making clouds of barrage balloons
once seen over a lake,
l would like to say St James' Park,
but it was probably Canberra,
bright and eucalyptus in the air
that pulls at me now, a year on, in seasons change,
in spite or because of the bell's toll,
sombre as council houses, counting passing hours,
too, too redolent with unrequited hopes,
possibilities that have been wasted,
not for want of trying,
by happenstance, coincidence, accident and chance.

Exmoor

Hoar frost strangles
yew and larch, cock partridge, magpie
blue and black sinks in bird-sang coarse,
silent as crow in kidney, tongue and selvedge,
fat as purple, fat as Caesar, that struts the bare and empty tops
that fall, unfailing, to imagined sea-sun lit
from moors and tors, and this daybreak
another morning come too early
for a lamb, untimely taken,
breathless, yellow, still.

Moray Firth, April

herring gulls career white ash dashed,
from chimneys lashed by northern sea
wild spray and climbing wind,
to hills made lie recumbent stilled
in schiltron bleak array
but for lee of golden gorse worn bravely
in grey charge of formless clouds
that chase the battered remnants of my soul
scattered in the forest bleak retreat of senses,
in raven call of abandoned reason,
and all of loves-lost hopes
in strange and sudden chapel-silent pine
cry *Sanctuary, Sanctuary*, where there is found
only the sound of weeping.

Iona

Shall we tear each other's hearts apart,
shall we,
make strange our love drowning in rain
and tears.
Shall we weep alone breathing island, island,
must we
cling in the wet embrace of memory
and fears
Shall we, in deep harbour, put in for repair
and there
plumb our souls, take soundings
exiled
like St Columba for shedding blood, others, ours,
shall we,
shall we?

From the Lakes

I'll give you wandering lonely, Wordsworth,
cloudless I am found,
restless as a stoat in heat
and burrowed 'neath the cottage
wherein you and goodness knows who with whom
the dales rang o'er hills and dales
I will take this my Raphaelite beauty
and cause you such dismay
among the iris and black violets of our love
that daffodils will be a pale mockery
of such intensity.

A Visit to Cambridge

It would have been a nice declension
should the earnest, peddling fast
blonde, with wicker basket
and brake that cried in protest,
perhaps she has no boyfriend to fix it,
had smiled in her passing, catching my eye as she did
or I imagined, in the sad vanity of age,
still alert to memories of a time when a glance
held, three seconds, they say,
was more than a look,
as on the Tube that afternoon when another,
in fascination with her phone, caught me
in spare and open stare for a time
and archly raised her eyebrows as the train then pulled away.

Monmouth

A pheasant, he pheasant,
cock pheasant struts,
shimmers green
and gold in beaten armour,
amour breasted bold,
in cock-hatted lust
in bead-eyed sheen,
stammers, coughs
love me, have me,
for you are mine
hen, hedgerow, field,
yield to me, you must,
look at me,
am I not fine, enough.

By a valley church,
sometime later
beside a quiet road, stands
a Morris dancer,
top hat, ribbons,
face blackened, eyes white,
belled legged,
stockings red leans
against a stone wall,
watches, me,
the laneway coppice,
smokes, coughs.
Curiouser and curiouser,
said Alice.

Above the gorse

echo rings
a hawk, mournful
shrieks wild tonal grief
loss, alack, alas, alas,

stops

silent

wings spread in embrace
borne mute
to where death calls,
waits,

and strikes
aphonic,
beyond sight

*'If it were done when 'tis done,
Then 'twere well…done quickly.'*

The Dead Mole

so much smaller than my expectation,
presented in the cup of a palm,
eyes blind, tender hands pink, a tiny snout
and skin like velvet caught hard in a trap
just behind the shoulders crushing ribs,
hearts, lungs, his fault a pursuit of earth moving
in simple endeavours,
mounds, in familiar straight lines,
corrupting hayfields,
despoiling pristine lawns
and for this he is abused, hunted,
condemned and killed,
a reaction, in my eyes,
disproportionate for such misdemeanours.

Passing Traffic

Ifor Jones Trailers,
Mansell Davies Sons & Stock Feed,
Brian Williams Posts, Wire,
Potting Mix and Charcoal,
Chorus,
Land of Our Fathers
Herds, calf, cow, bull,
alto, tenor, bass,
clothes lines full, chapels empty,
laneways choked, bar stools idle,
and caravan windows catch
flight path vapours,
the last peach sky racing clouds,
as worker wasps dash,
drunk on summer fruit,
spoiling for a fight like Swansea boys,
as the last of season's wool
fills the shed with early autumn snow.

Skoma Island

genus Fratercula:
Black and white plumage resembling monastic robes.
Puffin:
Middle English. The cured carcasses of nestling Shearwaters.

Come, you hilarious clowns,
my little brothers, uncloistered,
boldly drawn and carnival painted,
show me your idiot flight,
your clumsy colour-laden circus
of mating heat and staggering walk
windswept reckless in Atlantic gales,
a Groucho mask festooned with herring
makes Shrovetide revelry on blasted heath.

Passing the Baptist Chapel

This is the abyss again,
forever fate,
this forever, destiny,
the catalogue of mistakes,
the sum of hurt and pain
manufactured, carelessly,
hell mocking like Dante's Gates,
the black between earth and sky,
the fields and the stars,
opened to rains
sheet winds, bleak as heaven's
God dark voice, sonorous,
grey as chapel steps,
staggered as headstones
gathered among weeds tight
faint-headed gossamer,
wasted blue and rosemary,
for remembrance.

The Maiden Ewe

unseasonally fat, swollen-titted
presented a breech and twisted lamb,
restrained by youthful pelvic girdle
and disinterest common in the young,
to be pulled to ground by intervention,
yellow and unsteady, greeted air like a landed fish
in brief, infrequent spasms, cleaned
of hooded membranes, slapped, swung,
dropped hard in resurrection to, at last, find legs,
balance of a kind necessary for suckling,
sucking at life in the shallows of lung beat.

Laugharne

The estuary takes flight in snatches
catches light, dances, flirts,
as gentle ebb-tide waves
drift, drop soft sand
between rocks and marsh grass tresses,
floating tender as Ophelia
under blue sky gulls cry
Alas, Alack,
that circle ruins and turrets dreams,
above safe harbours cockled, smuggled,
tight as narrow lanes winding
past Brown's Hotel,
Guinness dark, shell bright,
from shining hills to river's edge.
Of Dullen there is little sign.

Carmarthen to Llandeilo

Time hangs in a drifting mist
unveiling, like a conjurer or lover,
the fleeting glimpse of sudden,
brilliant light, archangel bright, delighting green fields,
shining rushed and tumbled stumbling streams,
gutter moss-green singing rocks,
hills sheep white, lambs yellow and pink as sun
lie above forest dark secrets ivy clad,
spilt randomly across stones, under bridges,
weeping into roads gravel littered,
dying in amber lit fog village streets
at evening's close.

Wool Pressing, Wales

'Who calls me?'

'I do.'

Why? What have you there,
my strange and crippled man,
more wool to break my heart
with careless harvest, types in disarray,
black, and grey in hidden sheets
by cunning far too simple to succeed?

'A few speckled, some Mules. No Welsh.'

Liar.
For forty pence a kilo
you will torment me with such deceit,
hold your rotten bags tight with strings,
slyly knotted,
or twine, or splintered wooden pegs
once carefully shaped?
What local mill contrives them,
or an artisan, perhaps, more skilled
than you, my friend.

'Just the three sheets is it?'

'Aye, aye.'

Brilliant.

Cymru Bull

Bellow,
cry deep and shocking,
collect pain and anger
to dismay ghosts rib deep,
rent and echo
valley tops, rivers drop,
weep hurt and rage
at passing clouds song.
Bellow,
in fields vacant, lanes
caught, left undone
in summer's passing swift
merry green and berry hedges,
sad, corrupted flowers
on steep hills fall
into streams fast rush
meeting soft rains chorus.
Bellow
after the heifers, taken,
shake the gathered mist,
rolling dragon's breath,
call kings and magicians,
fill rowan trees bright with music,
bring sounds of sacrifice,
and ring bells
in sun's faint light,
such is your regret.

Finding the Words

I describe my *urgent* love
in italics the King's translators used
as they struggled for meaning
in the body of the psalms,
made three words five,
misread the essence,
but fearing to be clumsy
used a get-out clause,
a scholarly slight of hand,
an admission of defeat
they could not match the majesty,
so I must write *all* my love
in such fashion
for words are not made
that measure this passion.

Love is casual,
OED 1. Subject to, or produced by chance;
accidental, fortuitous.
2. Coming at uncertain times;
Not to be calculated on, unsettled 1460.
3. Occurring without design 1667.

skun of meaning,
flayed and now flaw'd
the word, the meaning
lies on the drying rack
beside the killing pen,
mapped with red veins,
drying in the sun,
twitching with the nervous memory
of dying, *'to pine away with passion'*.
I wipe the sticky mix of blood across my shirt,
the spectacularly prescient meat-ants
tracking across my boots,
love, a cross I have to bear.

Navigating love
I am adrift on a sea
legs entwined in muscle memory
that is not of my making
a tangle of Leda and the Swan
my moral compass
breathe in, breathe out
has been washed overboard
toe to toe, skin to skin
and I cannot find landfall.

Love is speechless
although it conspires to be so much more
than gaze or fleeting touch,
it makes itself bold,
brazen, *fig. Hardened in effrontery. 1573*
but in essence silent, without words,
simple shared breath and gentle tide
which, in sometimes rush of eager waves,
will bash an exultation
along cliffs of expectation, display,
candour, *1. Brilliant whiteness: 1692*
and subside quietly, honestly.

The Wombat Hole Reprise

'I'le goe hunt the badger by owle-light; tis is a deed of darkness' –
The Duchess of Malfi

i.

I could lose myself in these Welsh valleys,
run away, hide,
drown in rain and sky and winds
castellated downs,
dark awful forest snatches,
black-shattering grounds,
find an empty badger sett
cast on shale hill's tortured brows,
lie silent in shadows, breathless,
heart beating louder
than it must, should, would, can
and hear a gamekeeper's cannon
above the singsong cry of hounds
forced to heel,
as ripe uncommon airs
fill my head with mysteries
and tears swollen, spill, unexpected
in cloud scud eruptions beauty
where pieces of my heart,
spread like scat, will betray me.

ii. Hawthorn, The Bed-sit

This is not a proper burrow,
hole, *1. An excavation made for an animal.*
or haven, *2. fig. a refuge. OED*
it is a construct, like poetry
not yet hitting its rhythm
or rhyme,
an impermanent place
wherein it takes time
to manufacture periodicity
amongst the unfamiliar,
the coming and going,
the ever-present, the other
for which there is no map,
no familiar tracks, pads,
water points, no signs
for navigation in constant night light,
through bewildering labyrinth
and curious vacancy.

Coming Home

Welcome to Findon Street, Hawthorn,
not post-war British Brutalism in design,
the apartments that made The Elephant and Castle unlivable,
once vicious, dangerous,
that I passed on the 406 Waterloo bus,
taped-off, shut-up and empty,
bright with the only prospect renovation,
for this is Boyd's own Ugliness at its best.
Square. Red brick.
18 Apartments per,
cat-swinging space available
for a collection of ghosts
that cook, run showers, hawk, cough, fart,
flush toilets and never appear,
although footsteps clack the stairs occasionally
and rubbish bins find their place at the gutter,
miraculously in neat green rows
beside cars that never leave their Resident Permit Only,
for the bedsit is alive and well in this country,
although they may be called
Student Accommodation,
Studio Apartments,
Single Rooms Available,
any metaphor will do.
Square. Red brick,
18 Apartments per,
clothes line space available
if you're quick,
the common laundry washes, spins, eats coins
that never reappear,

although slippers shuffle the stairs occasionally
and clothes find their place ranked with pegs,
miraculously in neat coloured rows
beside towels that never leave their right of occupation,
for communal living is alive and well in this country
although it may be called
High Density,
High Intensity,
Caged Production,
any metaphor will do.

Thunderstorms are

i

just are, come unusual, shatter
scatter, in sudden outrage, reality
or its constructs, such as they are,
is, become, indistinct,
blue black fury gods manufacture
to remind, whispered on the wind,
You are a man, Caesar, just a man.

ii

In early northern blusters
prehensile cranes beyond the river
align with the wind,
as once the tails of windmills did,
and a half-moon, faint in the east,
rests like an upturned cup,
and rain will come tonight,
a trick of knowledge learnt while droving,
rain black tea-leaved and milky brown
to wash the streets
with sadly familiar grit.

iii

Carelessly abandoned
Violet spring sky fades
in wildcrack thunders scintillation
echoes, rattles ill-fitted windows,
catches blinds set to half-sail,
fills gutters with carousing song,
rolls in lightning's conjunction
howling wind, dogs, trees
bent in supplication,
bent begging absolution.

Today

clammy morning day cold grey,
  southerly winded harsh dark grief,
    a four of cockatoos wing close above,
      broad-shouldered angels sharp as sheets,
                maus-o-leum bright
                              white as fresco's wash
      discordant in their wailing tune torn aimless
          in flight flapping failing fight
with gravity, gliding, landing light as feathers
in tree top victory yellow-crested heralding
    a timid sun as once their cousins,
black, red, raucous were harbingers of rain
      in rare and lonely
          pairs.

The boy has his hair in a bun

He wears a paisley shirt. He reads a book,
With his sunglasses on
Even tho' it is overcast.

A girl with red hair in a bun
Sits opposite. Her sunglasses
Are on her head.
She reads a book.

Surely the irony is worth a smile.

Another boy gets on the tram.
He is wearing a printed T-shirt.
Underneath the logo it says,
BOY.

But we already knew.

A crippled man gets on
And checks in his travel card.
His T-shirt does not say
CRIPPLE.

It is quiet but for the wind.

The red-haired girl has long,
Long eyelashes and a black bra,
Straps sudden
Against her milk-white skin.

Another girl gets on.
She is blonde enough and obvious
And BOY looks
And combs his hair with his left hand.

The tram slows to a stop.

The first boy talks to the girl.
The girl talks to the first boy
And they get off.
She has a short skirt and long legs.

BOY steals another glance,
At the blonde.
She is checking her phone
So he looks out the window.

I am writing.

And then the second girl stares at me
But only briefly.
I am writing. I am odd,
but not odd enough for her.

The tram stops outside a church
and a fat man gets on.
His shirt does not, sadly, unfortunately, say
FAT.

Melbourne, The CBD

They come, they come,
they come in orderly, earnest waves,
like sheep that, having walked into the wind
reach the southern fence stop,
turn, and hurry back,
grey, dark and uniform
they lack the dash of colour fleeting
as parrots through the scrub,
a smile rarer still than kelpies grin.
At the corner of King and Collins,
the Brack regiments, black and black,
passing women but vague distractions,
merely swept along by heat and noise
in labyrinthine towers glass and steel,
by the shocking bell bell bell
a shrike constructs overhead
drowning bus, truck, trams,
in solo so arresting, notes so profound
they fall strewn, brief, shiny
as uncommon summer hail
onto tides below
that lack the acuity to hear or listen.

The butt end of a bronze and desiccated limb
lay in the gutter shaded by tall and stately planes,
not a palm tree in sight.
Had it fallen from the sky like Icarus,
caught the violence of a westerly change,
dropped from a passing avian,
a large one, a condor perhaps, blown off-course
from Chile, a long way from the Andes to Melbourne
to be carting a stupid piece of tree, worthless,
too big for nesting, unless condors make very big nests,
which they might.
Ask Isabella Allende, she'll know,
she deals in magic, or will at least make something up,
an answer.
My friend lifts it, feather light, although no threat
to passing traffic, deposits it in a nearby bin,
he is Malaysian, which explains a lot,
and it rests in an impromptu body bag with coffee cups,
chip packets, gum, and other butts,
the severed joint pointing to the sky.

Sparrows here now rare,
once handmaidens to Aphrodite,
harbingers of death, takers of the soul,
overwhelmed by immigrants, apparently.
A woman sits on a steel green bench,
sobs in shallow wracking breaths,
her clothes mismatched,
hair unkempt, a face ravaged, smokes,
the warm breeze, portent of coming heat
strokes her, carries away the exhalation,
wisps of sadness and despair no one sees
carries above the trees a departing spirit,
swept into the gods, and gone.
I do not stop, I am a lesser man,
sparrows bouncing at her feet.

In September

I bounce

I bounce the sherrin

I bounce the sherrin the footpath
still warm beneath bare feet
and it comes back in muscle memory,
spins in my hands
in the empty street,
in the full moon of once might have been
the training lights
of country grounds
as if it was years ago, take a screamer,

and wonder if in time
the ball will deflate, like me.

Outside are odd things

      Night birds,
           Owls,
                raptors whistle
And shrill,
          Again.
Or rats, perhaps,
A possum
Caught in talon's spear,

A cicada caught in hiatus,
Bats,
Maybe fruit bats, large bats squeal
Left behind
    by
                a squadron
colouring the sky in flocks of notes,
regular as black
notes, too many notes
For,
        moonlit dark bloodlust,
Descending,
Not my notes,
    Not
          my
                familiar
                      sounds,

The ones a life notated
A country ago, elsewhere,
A place of imagination
Wide as evening sky
       Fixed,
                  constant as sorrow, regret,
      Common as breathing.

Along the Yarra

A brief moment of panic,
no pen, no pencil to be found,
am I now so defined
although once, in another age, mustering sheep
left a note scratched with blackened match
on the wafer of cigarette paper, stuck into a gatepost,
'this paddock is clear move on to 9 mile',
I digress.

Two signs I would copy, on river bank,
in the gathering of saplings, grass in flower
where McCubbin may have easily lost his child,
DANGER
Jumping From this Bridge An Offence
MINIMUM FINE $200.
Is there a scale for jumping from a bridge,
a judge employed to adjudicate by local council?

I digress.
The other sign reads, read,
DANGER
Low Oxygen levels
& Sudden Rises in Water Level
and I knew straightway this was the place for me,
where I was meant to be, am.
I digress.

Victoria Gardens, Abbotsford

O temple of Mammon
You stand light, bright, seductive
In vast arcades of songs and feasting,
An indolent, aimless goddess spread
On her back
Wide-thighed, accommodating,
Embrace me,
The rows of money changers,
The high priests of sacrifice
Accepting offerings,
The bread and the circuses,
And you, you are
A whore, by any other name.

The Yarra Bank

The barmaid, was, too young to know,
as we,
hatted,
bald,
strutted duffle coat,
tweed-hatch jacket,
drunk in company,
drunk by pint spilt
stories careless as foaming glass
falling on coasters,
the river, out of sight, just,
the sun collapsing night too early,
said,
we said, emboldened,
It's OK,
We are poets
and the barmaid, too young to know
in black skirt, white blouse
mopping tables replied,
Are you?
Really? Poets?
bringing us, briefly,
to ground.

For my nephew

Young men write of other things,
witty, obscure, clever things,
concepts, ideas, in script and layout
like turned cuffs and Windsor knots,

clever
        Things.
                        See John and Janet run
see how clever I
            am.
But
one
day they may see
            that the life they know

        is not life yet, really,
or   wisdom
                        because that
                                comes
with age
        and thebearingofpaintheycannot
imagine.   Yet.

The Crossing

Waiting for dawn's yellow burst,
in nightfall evening's crisp sky
vacant, starless, pale brown
the river penleigh wattled,
Kane's Bridge painted, still, hung,
creaks and hovers, cable strung,
as in my youth.
Why here was made a crossing,
in this pregnant belly swollen bend
when in short sight upstream,
downstream, begs brief enough fords
for my cattle, even sheep,
to walk horse and foot,
madly enough elephant on barges?
Odd. I suspect it was the Victorians,
in their largesse and conceit,
having once seen Albert's Memorial.

Studley Park Night-time

The raining pixilates
the windscreen cracked in low horizon
runs not quite its length,
gut-busted by the strike of bird,
leaks, and drips persistent, falls
in drops
irregular
as heartbeat,
while the traffic comes and goes
like fireflies in tail-lit
light flit catch the dark, in brief trysts,
uncomplicated by the hour,
the evening not yet grey as dreams,
or clear as hopes,
as shining clouds that race
and catch the moon in quick meter.

Horse Riding for the Disabled. Carpe Diem

Once abandoned,
shunned, exorcised, cast as demons,
cast aside, now saddled in spite of,
now in giggling delight,
in anticipation, anxiety,
fearless, for the senate declares
soon they will be gods,
centaurs,
that smile, wave,
and are generous in the distribution of their favours
as befits one who is led,
and escorted,
acolyte at each thigh.
These caesars need not mortality,
they have not seized the day,
they have translated correctly,
embraced the moment.

First Placement in Aged Care

The collection of souls arranged,
(an exhibition of Freud's,
Lucien,
once seen in the safety
of The National Portrait Gallery
London,
which stains me still,
or descriptions Hogarth engraved,
viewed in storied
Georgian clutter earlier,
or was that before?)
in composition of figures flung
by life's vagaries into distress,
decline, forgetfulness
that mark the constant ebb and flow
of toilet, dressing, eating, sleeping
toilet, the same, the same
familiar or unremembered,
that circular repetition not light nor night
can unravel,
or if it did, to what end?

Those who know are bravest,
Olive, Olga,
cutched up like Ötzi
the Copper Age shepherd
who knew his time had come, resigned
to fading light, gathering snow,
uncomplaining,
skun of nightclothes barely covered
by flesh my agents would have not considered
if offered on the bones of old mutton,
unseemly restricted amongst their like
to be pushed and prodded,
rolled off their arse, washed,
weighed,
knowing that this, too, will pass,
but of sufficient dignity to say,
Yes please.
Thank you, dear.
That'll be nice.

www.ingramcontent.com/pod-product-compliance
Lightning Source LLC
Chambersburg PA
CBHW062141100526
44589CB00014B/1653